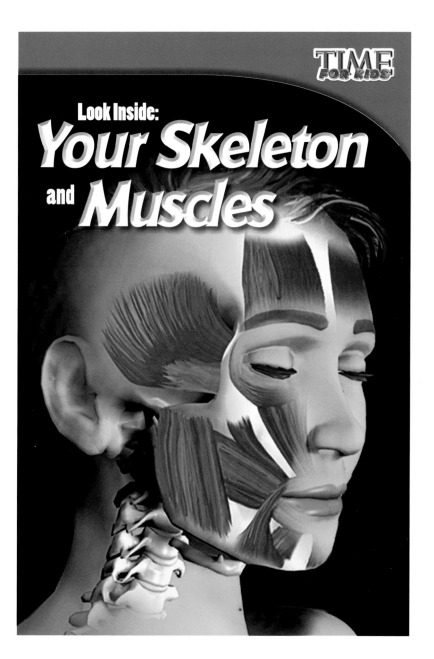

TIME
FOR KIDS

Look Inside:
Your Skeleton
and *Muscles*

Ben Williams

Consultant

Timothy Rasinski, Ph.D.
Kent State University

Publishing Credits

Dona Herweck Rice, *Editor-in-Chief*
Robin Erickson, *Production Director*
Lee Aucoin, *Creative Director*
Conni Medina, M.A.Ed., *Editorial Director*
Jamey Acosta, *Editor*
Stephanie Reid, *Photo Editor*
Rachelle Cracchiolo, M.S.Ed., *Publisher*

Teacher Created Materials

5301 Oceanus Drive
Huntington Beach, CA 92649-1030
http://www.tcmpub.com

ISBN 978-1-4333-3635-5
© 2012 Teacher Created Materials, Inc.

Table of Contents

The Skeleton and Muscles

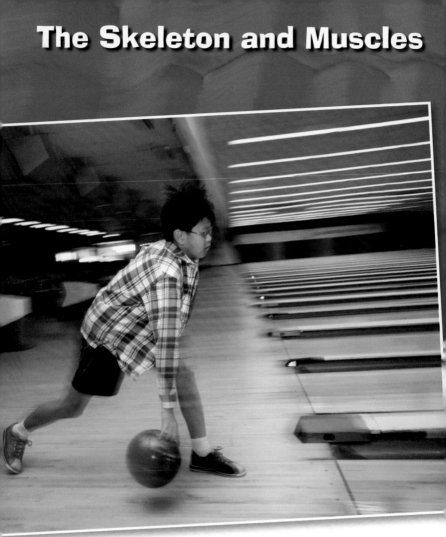

Imagine if you had no **skeleton** or **muscles** (MUHS-uhls). How would you stand? How would you move?

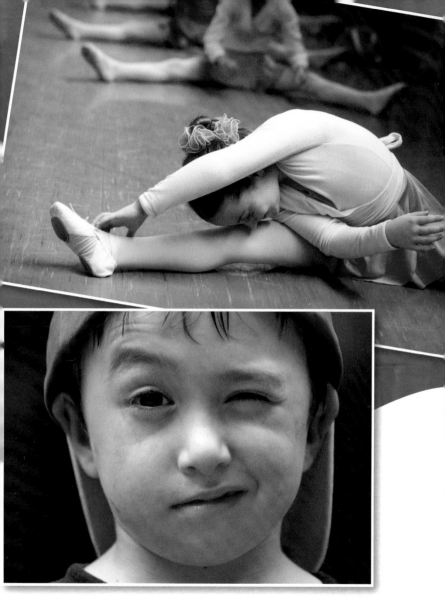

How would you throw a ball, touch your toes, or even blink your eyes?

The answer is that you could not do any of those things. You need a skeleton and muscles to do all the things you want to do.

Your skeleton and muscles work
together. They help you keep your shape
and allow you to move.

All About the Skeleton

If you look at yourself in the mirror, you can get a good idea of what your skeleton is like under your skin.

Bones are inside every part of your body. Bones connect to make your skeleton, and your skeleton gives you your size and shape.

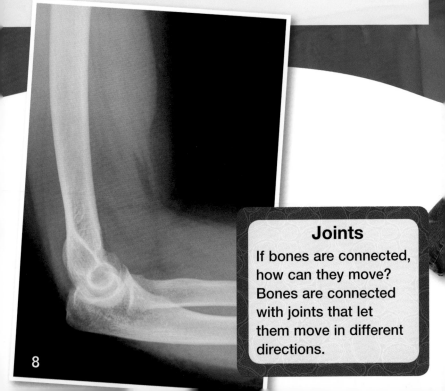

Joints

If bones are connected, how can they move? Bones are connected with joints that let them move in different directions.

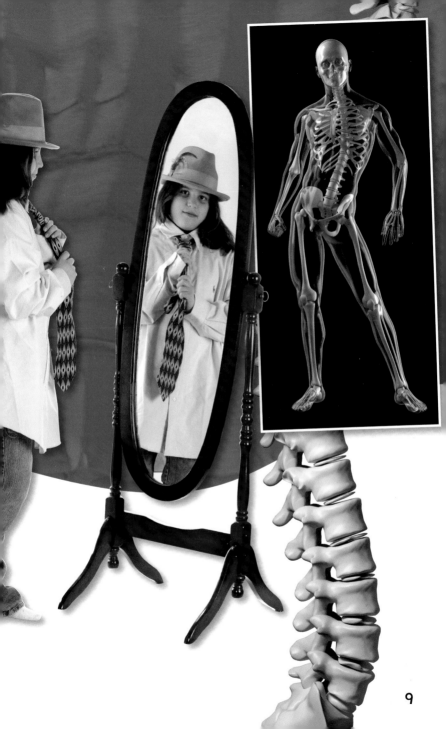

Each bone in your body has its own important job to do.

Some bones protect you. Your skull is one of those bones. It protects your brain.

Some bones give you shape. Your ribs make the shape of your chest. They protect your heart, lungs, stomach, and liver, too.

Some bones give you strength to stand. Your femur (FEE-mer) is the thigh bone. It helps to hold you up.

Amazing!
If bones are broken, they can grow together again.

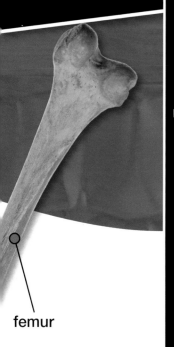

femur

Skull Bones

The skull looks like one bone, but it is really made of 28 bones. The skull bones connect like the pieces of a puzzle.

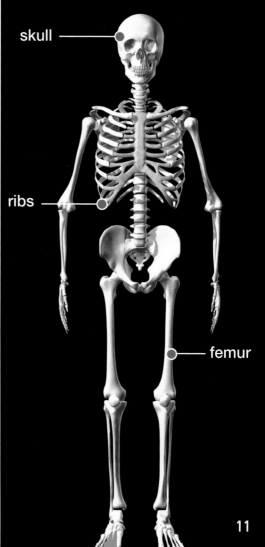

skull

ribs

femur

11

Bones do something else that is very important. They help to make your blood.

Inside each bone is marrow. It is soft like jelly. Bone marrow makes new blood for your body.

Bone marrow also stores **nutrients** (NOO-tree-uhnts) for the body.

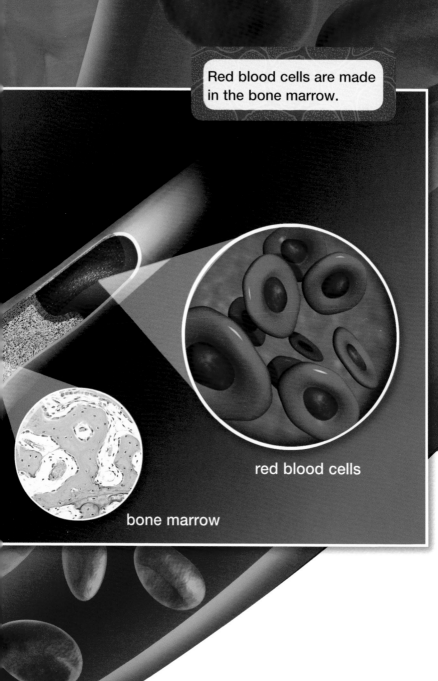

Red blood cells are made in the bone marrow.

red blood cells

bone marrow

Bones may be soft on the inside, but they are hard on the outside. They are made from some of the same things you can find in rocks! These things are called **minerals**.

Bones are also dry compared to the rest of the body. A large part of your body is made of water, but only a small part of your skeleton is.

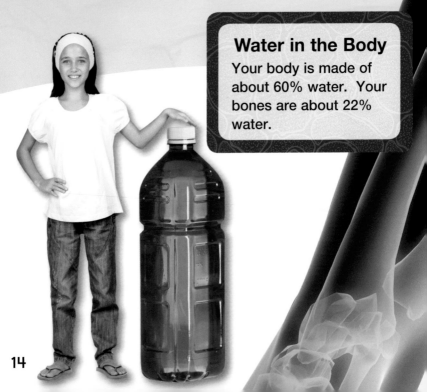

Water in the Body
Your body is made of about 60% water. Your bones are about 22% water.

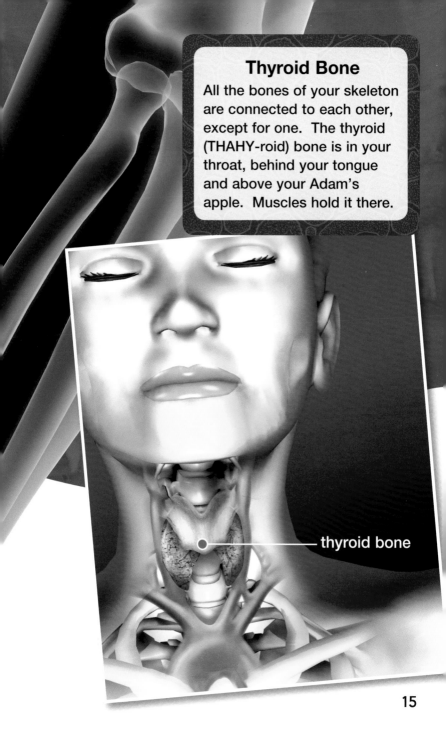

Thyroid Bone

All the bones of your skeleton are connected to each other, except for one. The thyroid (THAHY-roid) bone is in your throat, behind your tongue and above your Adam's apple. Muscles hold it there.

thyroid bone

As you grow older, your body grows bigger. You get more of almost everything as you grow: more teeth, more hair, more height, and more weight.

But, you do not get more bones. In fact, you get fewer!

Smallest and Biggest

The smallest bone you have is in your ear. It is called the *stapes* (STEY-peez), and it helps you hear. The biggest bone you have is the femur in your thigh. (See page 11 for a picture of a femur.)

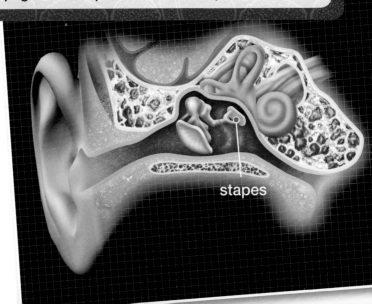

stapes

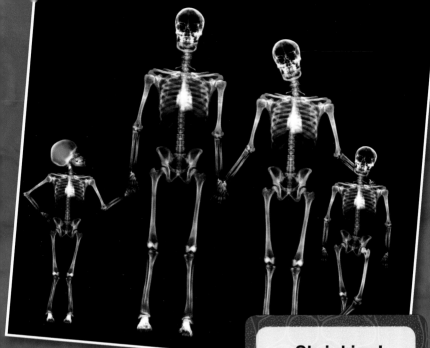

Most bones grow longer and bigger as you grow older, but some bones also grow together into one big bone. So, even though a baby has more than 300 bones, an adult has only 206 bones.

Shrinking!

You are shorter at night than you are in the morning! During the day, **gravity** causes the bones in your back to close the spaces between them, so you shrink a little. At night, the spaces soak up water, making you taller again.

All About Muscles

Which of these body parts are made mostly of muscles?

- tongue
- heart
- lips
- stomach

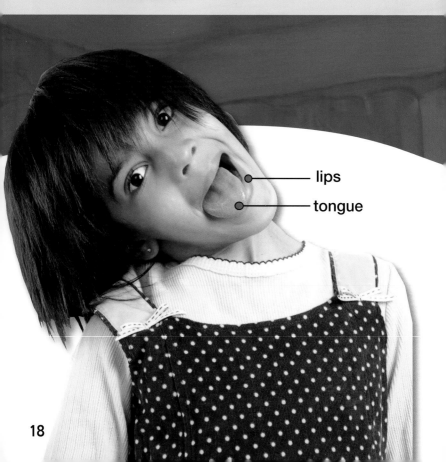

lips

tongue

heart

stomach

Can you guess? The answer is all of them! They each have many muscles that help them do their jobs. Without muscles, they would just lie there and do nothing at all.

What exactly are muscles? They are the parts of the body that move bones and make body organs like the heart, lungs, and stomach work. They are also in the walls of **blood vessels** to make blood move.

There are more than 650 different muscles in your body. That is a lot! Your muscles make up a little less than half of your total weight. So, if you weigh 60 pounds, your muscles weigh about 25 pounds.

Smile!
Did you know that it takes more muscles to frown than to smile?

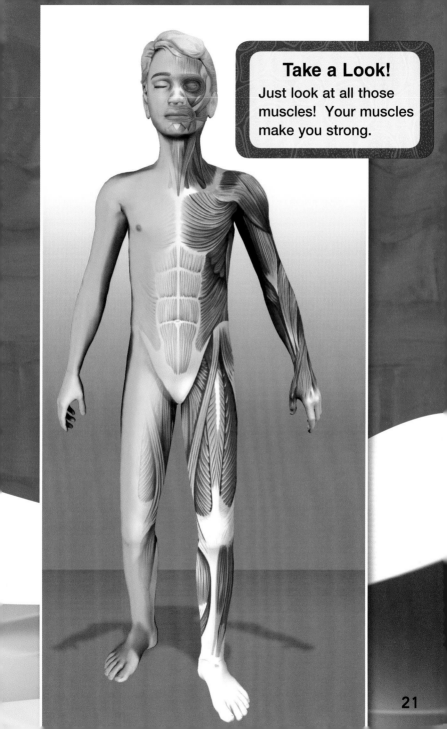

Muscles are made of hundreds or thousands of thin strands called *fibers* that can stretch and snap back into shape, a little like a rubber band does. This lets you move your bones in many different ways.

smooth muscle fibers

There are three main types of muscles: smooth, cardiac, and skeletal. **Smooth muscles** are mostly in body organs and some blood vessels. They do things for your body without you thinking about them, like digest your food and move your blood.

Cardiac (KAHR-dee-ak) **muscles** are in the heart. They make your heart pump.

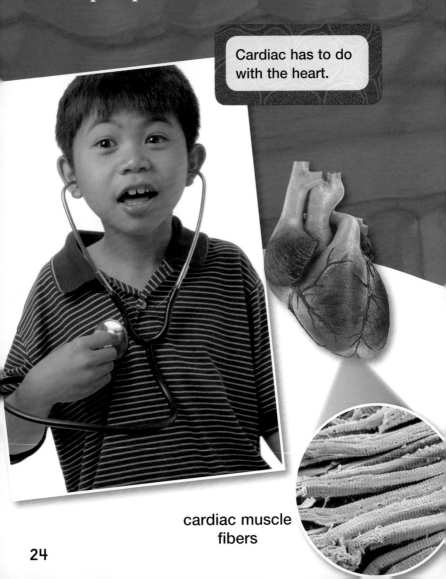

Cardiac has to do with the heart.

cardiac muscle fibers

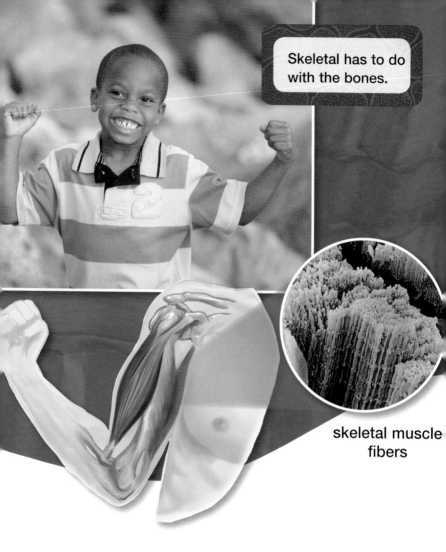

Skeletal has to do with the bones.

skeletal muscle fibers

Skeletal (SKEL-i-tl) **muscles** are connected to bones. You use them to move things like your legs, arms, neck, and fingers.

Building Strong Bones and Muscles

How do bones and muscles grow and become stronger? Exercise makes them grow and keeps them fit. The more you use them, the stronger they are and the more energy they have.

You should exercise every day. You can exercise just by playing. Jumping and running are two great ways to keep your bones and muscles strong and healthy.

Strong!

What is your strongest muscle? It is the jaw muscle. It gets exercise every time you eat or talk.

jaw muscle

Your bones and muscles need good food, too. Good food keeps them strong and helps them to last a long, long time.

Hefty!

Muscles allow you to lift heavy things. The most weight any human being has ever lifted is 6,270 pounds. A man named Paul Anderson did that in 1957.

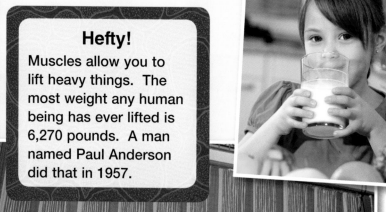

Glossary

blood vessels—the tubes that run through the body to carry blood to and from the heart

cardiac muscles—the muscles in the heart that make your heart pump

gravity—an invisible force that holds people and other objects on Earth

minerals—the combinations of atoms and molecules that form the basic parts of rocks, bones, and other parts of the body

muscles—the parts of the body that move bones and make body organs

nutrients—something in food that helps people, animals, and plants live and grow

skeletal muscles—the muscles connected to your bones

skeleton—the bones of a human or animal that are connected together

smooth muscles—the involuntary muscles located throughout the body